101 Ways to Talk to

GOD

101 Ways to Talk to GOD

Dandi Daley Mackall

SOURCEBOOKS, INC.
NAPERVILLE, ILLINOIS

Published by Sourcebooks, Inc.
P.O. Box 4410, Naperville, Illinois 60567-4410
(630) 961-3900
FAX: (630) 961-2168

Library of Congress Cataloging-in-Publication Data

Mackall, Dandi Daley
101 ways to talk to God / by Dandi Daley Mackall
   p. cm.
   ISBN 1-57071-636-6 (alk. paper)
   1. Christian life. 2. Spiritual life I. Title: One hundred and one ways to talk to God II. Title: One hundred one ways to talk to God. III. Title.

BV4501.2 .M2375 2001
248.3—dc21

                                                     00-066168

Printed and bound in the United States of America

               PX 10 9 8 7 6 5 4 3 2 1

Dedication

For Don & Catharine Mansfield,
who talk to God all the time

A Secret Gift

Give something away anonymously—to someone who would NEVER suspect you were the giver. It could be a plant, a service (like mowing a yard), fresh oranges, or money. Thank God for the gifts you've received when you least expected to—a phone call from a friend, a card, an unexpected ray of sunshine, a sense of God's presence.

Forgive Someone

Prayerfully bring before God someone who has wronged you, gossiped or lied to or about you, or broken a promise. Write God a letter giving away every pain, treachery, injustice, disappointment, or hurt feeling this someone has done to you. Tear up the letter and toss it in the trash. Choose to forgive.

Thank God for forgiving you.

Lone Whisper

Be the only person at a sporting event to talk with God (about something other than a win!). Pick the most intense point in the game; amid the loud cheers, whisper to God. Tell God you appreciate the fact that, even in a crowd, God is right beside you, just a whisper away.

Finding Light

When you need to make a major decision,
find someplace where you can be alone in
complete darkness. Talk to God about your
options. Be still and listen for God's answer.
Ask for light in the darkness.

Plant a Miracle

Plant a garden, a tulip, or a tree. Dig in
the dirt. Imagine what your bulb or seedling
will look like in one year, in ten years, in
one hundred years! Meditate on God's miracle
of growing things. Thank God for growing you.

Share a Sunrise with God

Watch the sun come up over an ugly spot—a deserted lot, an abandoned factory, a crowded parking lot, a no-zoning strip. Imagine God sitting next to you, sharing the moment. Pay attention to the changes in the sky, and look for patches of loveliness—the way the sun glints off a piece of broken glass, the warming rays that stretch over the cold pavement. Ask God to give you glimmers of hope, even in ugly circumstances. Finish your day by joining God for a sunset over your favorite place.

Spiritual Scrubbing

Clean something thoroughly—a tub or a desk, under beds, or inside cupboards. As you watch the transformation, thank God for cleansing your soul. Give God any secret shame that haunts you, a past mistake you've tried to cover up. Accept the gift of newness of life with God, of starting with a clean slate.

8

Doctor's Office Offering

If you find yourself stuck in the doctor's or dentist's
office, instead of reading old magazines,
have a healthy conversation with God. Now is
the time to thank God for all the things that
are *right* about your health and body. You also
might need to thank God for certain weaknesses
that have made you depend on God more.
Talk over any fears you have about life, illnesses,
and death. Nobody knows more about your
body than God—not even your doctor.

Embrace God's Power

Next time there's a storm (with no threat of
lightning!), run outside and let the storm swirl
around you. Feel the force and strength. As you
do, recognize God's incredible power! Embrace
God as the power behind the universe.

Share Your Fears

Share with a close friend a specific fear
that is holding you back from success—from
asking for a promotion, from taking that new
job or leaving one, from committing to another
person. Then pray together, or ask for prayer.
As an act of loving companionship, in a spirit
God would cherish, then offer to listen to your
friend's fears and to give prayerful support.

Enjoy the Moment

Take a walk on the street you live on or in a park
you know well. Pay attention to the details—the
combinations and shades of color in yards, the
way light inside houses spills onto lawns, the
smoke rising from chimneys, the buds and
flowers. If you can't "smell the roses," try to
detect scents you usually ignore. Ask God to
help you slow down, to do a double-take
and appreciate everyday blessings.

Make a Gratitude Album for God

Take a roll of pictures of things you're grateful for—a tree, the sky, friends and family, your bed, the view from your porch or window, your tomato plants. Put all your photos into a Gratitude Album for God, giving silent thanks as you assemble the pages. You might want to write under each picture why this individual or object makes you grateful.

Make a Lunch Date with God

Make a lunch date with God. No one else will
know except for you and God. As you're eating
your lunch, give God the same attention you
might offer a boss at a business lunch. In your
mind, discuss work relationships, business
dealings, plans, and prospects.

14

Finding God in a House of Worship

Go to church or temple, and save a seat for God!
Secretly pretend that you're singing each hymn as
a solo, with God as your only audience. Expect
God to speak to you through someone else,
through lyrics, or in your own thoughts.

Seek Out a Godly Example

Dig into your past and single out someone who has set a godly example for you. Think of a person you admire because of his or her strength of character—a teacher who turned you on to poetry or coaxed you through algebra, a brother-in-law devoted to his wife and children. Write a letter and let that person know how God has used him or her in your life. Thank God for this person, and ask for help in being a godly example yourself.

Pass On Your Love of God

Ask God to give you boldness and a sincere faith.
Then tell one other person today that you love God.
Be prepared to say why. (And be prepared to be
teased.) Pass along your good feelings about God.

Make Up a God Song

Make up a song for God—a song of thanksgiving,
a song of praise, a sad song, or a love song.
Use a favorite tune and write new lyrics, or
create your own melody. Sing your original
God Song, adding verses whenever you like.

Make the World Better

Pick your biggest complaint or criticism about the world—the condition of the homeless, violence, the state of the youth in America, racism, the polluted environment. Respectfully complain about the problem to God. When you have your complaints off your chest, ask God what you can do to be part of the solution—Help out in a soup kitchen? Volunteer at the youth rec center? Pick up a stretch of public beach? Get involved in local politics? Do more than complain.

Discover God in a Zoo

Go to the zoo and watch monkeys, elephants, seals,
birds, giraffes, lions, and bats. Allow yourself to be
amazed by the diversity of animal life and the
Creator who could think up such creatures.
Imagine the Creator walking through the zoo with
you. Compliment God's handiwork.

Share a Psalm with God

Read the 23rd Psalm aloud. After each line, make up
a line of your own, or say the thought in your
own words. Speak the psalm back to God.
Try the same "dialogue" with other Psalms.

"The Lord is my Shepherd."
You are my bodyguard when I ride home alone at night.

"I shall not want."
*Help me not to obsess about getting
my raise or promotion.*

"He makes me lie down in green pastures."
*I'm grateful for my front porch, back yard,
and the solace of a long drive.*

Finish the Psalm with God.

Three-Way Conversation

Talk to a friend about the unanswered, eternal
questions, as well as the things you know for
sure. Be free to say what you really believe—
about creation, about God's will, about good and
evil. Allow your friend to do the same. Begin
and end your conversation by talking to
God together. Thank God for your friendship
and God's love for both of you.

Alphabet Praise

Think of something great about God, beginning
with each letter of the alphabet. (A—Adoring or
Always near; B—Best friend or Brilliant;
C—Caring or Creative; D—Dependable or Deeper
than I can go;....) Continue your praise
through the entire alphabet.

Make God Your Companion

Take a walk in rotten weather. Laugh at the drizzle,
the blizzard, or the mud puddles. Thank God
for sticking with you—when you lost your
love, when the job fell through, when you totalled
your car, or tapped out your life's savings. You
will understand that you don't have to walk
alone through your adversities—
disappointments, failures, illness, death.

Say "I Love You" to God in another Language

If you feel as if your love for God has grown cold, try saying "I love you" to God in different languages. As you do, listen to the sound of the syllables (even if you mispronounce them!). Let your heart speak the words your mind might not understand:

Je t'aime (French)

Nhebuk (Arabic)

Yes Kez si'rumem (Armenian)

Ya Tyebya lyublyu (Russian)

Ek is lief vir jou (Afrikaans)

Te dua (Albanian)

Saranghaeyo (Korean)
Kocham cie (Polish)
Main tainu pyar karna (Punjabi)
Iniibig kita (Filipino)
Sizi seviyorum (Turkish)
Toi yeu em (Vietnamese)
Techihhila (Sioux)
Jien inhobbok (Maltese)
Ich hoan dich gear (Alsacien)
Mi aime jou (Cajun)
Jeg elsker dig (Danish)
Kimi o aishiteiru (Japanese)
Eu amo-te (Portuguese)
Annee ohev otakh (Hebrew)

Then thank the God who
understands all languages.

Turn the other cheek

The next time someone hurts your feelings with a
thoughtless or careless remark, take a deep breath.
Instead of returning the remark or getting angry,
smile and tell God it hurts. Then think of three
good things God would say about you—your
self-control, your patience, your kindness.
And for good measure, tell God three good
things about the other person.

Skip Rope With God

Ride a roller coaster, go night-sledding with a
flashlight, skip rope, play catch, swing, play
hopscotch, climb a tree...remember. Be a kid again.
Pretend God is going along with you, your best
buddy. Don't forget that God invented fun. Thank
him for it as you coast, skip, swing, and climb.

Shout out to God

When nobody's around (in a forest or in your living room), talk to God out loud. Shout the good stuff! Call out a hearty "Thanks, I love you! Awesome friend you've given me." Go on. Don't be shy.

The Blessings of Fall

Lie down under a tree during autumn and let the
leaves gently fall on you. Stare up through the
branches at the sky and listen to the silence and to
God. Take in the crunch of dried leaves, the touch,
smells, sounds, and sights of fall. Try to hear what
God is saying about the universe and about you.

Photo-Synthesize with Your Loved Ones

Collect pictures of people you know God has put in your life for a purpose. Paste a photo of your mom on the visor of your car, stick a favorite uncle on the fridge, post a niece on your dresser, or put a school friend in your desk drawer. When you run across the photos during your daily routine, talk to God about the people in your life. Ask for guidance for that niece or school friend, health for your uncle, joy for your mom.

Get a Hug from God

The next time you feel unloved, take time out to
cuddle a cat or hug a dog. Listen to the purr. Feel
the tenderness. Think about a God who wants to
hug you that close, who longs to comfort you,
and who delights in your nearness.

Reality Check

Retreat to a lonely spot and recall the goals
you have already accomplished—job, marriage,
family, education, travel, owning a house,
learning how to play tennis or the guitar.
Celebrate those accomplishments, and be
thankful. Tell at least one other person about
one goal realized. Give God credit!

The Blessings of Patience

Take on something you know makes you impatient—learn how to sew, tutor a child, teach an adult to read, walk a poky dog, ask a too-talkative person how he feels. Admit that complete patience is out of your reach. Ask God to help you grow in understanding. Thank God for the many ways God is patient with you.

God as Your Museum Guide

Imagine that God is walking through a museum
with you. Let yourself be amazed by what you see.
Share your reactions with God as you meditate
on the beauty and diversity of art. Ask God to
help you see art outside the museum, too—in
the uniqueness of strangers you pass in the
street, in buildings and designs, in the
shadows cast by sunlight through trees.

Let Your Mistakes Go Up in Smoke

Write down the ugly parts of your past—the regrets, the stupid acts you wish you had never done, the words you never should have spoken, things you wish you had done, mistakes that keep surfacing to haunt you. Talk to God. Confess each mistake one last time as you write it on your list. Then, tear your list into tiny pieces and burn them. As the smoke rises, thank God for forgiveness and fresh starts.

Open Your Heart With Music

Quietly listen to music you do not particularly
like. Country fans may opt for classical; rock
fans might try jazz; people who love the
classics might give rock a chance. As you listen,
try to understand why so many other people
enjoy this music. Contemplate how God created
different pleasures for different people, and
consider how you can enjoy them, too.

The Hard Way to Fresh Possibilities

Do something physically difficult. Run, swim, lift weights, or work out for one minute as hard and fast as you can. (Be sure your doctor has no objections!) Talk to God about the untapped resources you have been given in every area of your life—the potential to be a better parent or a more thoughtful child, the ability to be a more efficient worker or a better friend.

Open yourself to new possibilities.

candlelight Prayer

Light a candle and watch the brilliant flame.
Think about its effect on the darkness around
you, the way the glow reaches into far corners
and takes the fear out of the room. Contemplate
what it means that God is the Light of the World.
Talk with God about how you can reflect
God's light and drive away the dark feelings
you might have about others.

Whistle a Hymn to God

Try whistling or singing a hymn when you know you'll be drowned out to everyone but God. Whistle while you vacuum, sweep, or mow. Sing as you dust or rake leaves. Allow God to change the way you look at tasks that might seem to be dull.

Prayer Chair

Secretly designate one chair in your home as
your own, personal prayer chair. Imagine yourself
climbing into God's lap for a heart-to-heart.
Make an appointment with God to meet right
there every morning and every night. Start and
end your day in the lap of God.

Say "Yes"

Say "Yes!" to something you've always said "No!" to in the past. (Make sure it's not something God *wants* you to reject.) Go ahead—take a cruise, get a pet, agree to lead your Sunday school class, take your child to the circus, play catch, read Shakespeare.

Thank God that it's never too late to change.

Take Something Apart to Make Amends

Pull the petals off of a rose. Take apart an old clock. Now, try to put the petals back on or reassemble the clock. Meditate on how easy it is to destroy and tear down. Ask God to show you any harmful ways in your own dealings with other people—neglect, destructive criticism, a careless jest that might have hurt someone's feelings. If you've caused destruction, make amends.

Rewind a Year in Your Life

Turn off the TV and stare at the blank set. Picture
God sitting next to you. Rewind and let images
of the past year play in your head, as if you are
watching a movie of your life. Only, this movie
shows what was going on *inside* your mind,
too—your deepest thoughts, meanest attitudes,
insecurities, and true motives. Did you wish
failure on anyone you work with? Were you
insincere or inwardly hateful with people you
love? Talk over each scene with God. God already
knows your deepest thoughts...and still loves you!

Take a Drive with God

The next time you drive somewhere alone, use the time to pray for a meaningful, God-directed life. Talk over things, as if God were sitting in the passenger seat. Discuss what it means to let God steer your life and give you direction. What would it mean to allow God to accelerate or put the brakes on your plans? Determine to leave the driving to God.

Widen your World

Whenever you begin to believe that there's
nothing you need to talk to God about,
alert yourself to other people in trauma. When
you see a life-flight overhead, pray for the
person inside, for the family, and the medical
staff. When an ambulance races past
you, instead of reluctantly pulling over, talk to
God on behalf of the people involved.
Widen your discourse with God.

45

Drink in God's Spirit

Remind yourself, as you drink something cold on a hot day, that God's Spirit can quench your soul in the same way the drink quenches your thirst. On a cold day, drink something hot and let it warm you inside. Meditate on the way God's Spirit can soothe and calm you as you let him into every part of your being. Thank God for his refreshing Spirit.

Cook a Love Meal

Cook something for someone you love. Then cook
the same thing for someone you have trouble liking,
or someone easily ignored. As you cook and deliver
your selfless gift, talk to God about the many
selfless gifts God gives to you—a full moon, a flock
of honking geese, first buds on trees, the first
snowfall—even when you're not very loveable.

Holiday Prayer

Connect each holiday to God by talking to God first. Let God get the first "Happy New Year!" On Valentine's Day, tell God you love him first. When it's President's Day, talk to God about giving him the absolute power in your life. On April Fool's Day, ask for wisdom. Begin each holiday by applying the event to your relationship with God, and transform the day into a holy day.

48

Watch the Miracle of Birth

Arrange to observe something being born—a new
calf, a colt, a rabbit, a puppy. Experience and thank
God for the miracle of birth. Mull over the wonders
and miracles involved in bringing *you* into the
world. Talk to God about what else you could do to
make your life count—become involved in your
house of worship, give more of yourself to your
family, make a major career change.

Take God Fishing

If you're lucky enough to actually go fishing, do it!
You'll have hours to contemplate and talk to God.
As you relax and enjoy the process of fishing, talk
to God about what it means to enjoy the processes
in your life—the building of your home, and not
just the home itself; learning, not just graduating.
Ask God to help you find the minor joys of putting
a project together and progressing through it,
rather than just celebrating the end. Enjoy fishing,
even if you do not catch a fish.

Make Their Day

During one of your routine days, go out of your
way and imagine what God might do in your place
to make somebody's day. Give up a seat on the
subway or bus. Look for ways to be chivalrous.
Listen politely to the entire telemarketing pitch.
Compliment the waitress, the janitor, or the clerk
on the job well done. Let your kindness to others
speak to God, acknowledging your respect for the
people God's created and placed in your path.

51

Find God When You Are Lost

It will happen sooner or later…one day you'll be
driving and discover you're hopelessly lost. Instead
of reacting with anger or panic, realize that
even lost, you're not alone. Tell God how grateful
you are that God will always be with you, no
matter where you find yourself. Turn the
lost experience into an adventure with God
and a chance to find your way back with God.
Tell the feeling of hopelessness to "get lost!"

52

God Is Never on Hold

The next time you make a phone call and you're put on hold, or when you can't connect instantly to the Internet, hold on. Imagine that you have God on the line. What do you need to ask God in this brief, business-like phone call? Do you need good judgment in making a deal? Do you want wisdom and insight before you invest? Do you need a healthy dose of understanding before you talk with that employee? Ask. God won't put you on hold.

A New Flavor from God

The next time you bake cookies, make a cake, or cook dinner for friends, make preparation an act of prayer. Consider each simple ingredient and the way they combine to make a new taste. When your guests arrive and you serve them, observe the "ingredients" of your group and the new taste God provides when you come together.

Beautify God's World

Without telling anyone what you're doing, pick out
a neglected stretch of God's world—that ditch
across the road that collects debris, the constantly
littered shortcut from the high school, one end of
the park. Make it better—pick up litter, rake leaves,
scoop up pet mess. As you do your part, talk to
God, acknowledging the presence of God as you
beautify your piece of the world God created.

Comfort as You've Been Comforted

Thank God for all the ways God has comforted
you throughout your life—given you someone to
talk to when you were alone, protected you, made
you feel loved and worthy. Recall the friends and
relatives who have helped you through problems
by bringing you food when you didn't feel like
cooking, listening to you when you felt like talking,
getting you out of the house when you needed
a change of scenery. In return, give that same
kind of help to someone else—a phone call, a
visit, a gift, your presence. Picture God
beside you as you pass along comfort.

Count and Save Your Blessings

Make a list of blessings God has given you.
Keep going until you reach fifty. Don't forget
to include the little things—the smell of baked
bread and cut grass, the sight of a flock of
birds taking off, then suddenly changing direction.
Save your list. Pull it out on those days when
you feel everything is going wrong. Go through
the list, thanking God for each item. Then add
at least one more blessing to the list.

Join God in the Night Shift

The next time you find you can't sleep at night,
instead of fretting over your insomnia, welcome it
as an invitation to meet with God. Take the night
shift. As you enjoy the night sounds, the creaky
boards, shifting winds, and cricket calls, converse
with God. Talk over whatever is on your mind.
And pray for all your sleeping loved ones!

Tickle Someone You Love!

Select someone you love who could use a good tickle! Enjoy the laughter. Be prepared to be tickled back. Tell God how thankful you are to have people you can feel intimate with, people who like to laugh. Resolve to laugh more and to talk with God when things are going great, not just when you're down and feeling the need for God's companionship.

Remember a Grieving Friend

Talk to God about a friend who has lost someone he or she loves. Reach back farther than a year. Most people grieve long after their friends have stopped checking in on them. Write a card and let your friend know you're still praying and remembering. If it's appropriate, share a story or memory of the loved one. Ask God to help this person through the loneliness of loss.

Apologize to Someone

Humbly ask God to reveal to you anyone you
may have wronged, anyone whose feelings you
may have hurt. Don't stop praying until you have
the answer. Then prayerfully go to the person
(or write) and offer a sincere apology.
Ask forgiveness if you feel you need to, but
don't expect anything in return.

61

Bird Talk

If you're not a bird-watcher, become a bird-listener
for ten minutes. Sit outside, or camp out where
trees abound, and listen to the birds. Try to identify
their different songs, calls, and chirps. As you relax
to God's music, give thanks for these pleasure-
giving gifts. And try to learn a bird call or two,
imagining how the feathered friends talk to God.

See God in Your Rearview Mirror

When you stop at a red light and have to wait for the green, check yourself out in the rearview mirror. Stare into your own face and imagine you're face-to-face with God. Focus on one subject that is really on your mind. Reflect on the situation with God, eyeball-to-eyeball. And thank God that he's there for you in an instant, even at a stoplight.

Tell God About Your Anxieties

For most of us, uninvited anxieties show up regularly. We may forget to pray, but we never forget to worry—about our weight, our wrinkles, how we're doing at work, whether our loved ones are happy. Try using the automatic nature of worry to transform your prayer life. Use anxiety as a reminder. The instant a worry pops to mind, pray—pass your concerns on to God.

Hold a Mock Court Before God

Imagine walking into a court room to present your case before the court. Your case involves someone against whom you hold a grudge, a person who wronged or hurt you, or one who betrayed you or lied to you. Picture God as the judge who settles all accounts fairly. As if you are a lawyer, make your case against this person to God. Then leave the judgment and sentencing to the Judge. Exit the "court room," and let the bitterness go.

Use Your Library to Inspire Awe

Take a trip to the library and get a vision of God's astounding intelligence. Thumb through reference books on animal instincts and camouflaging. Read a biology book about the intricacies of the human body. Check out a book about an unfamiliar country and study its people and culture. Commend God on what you can deduce about him from these reference books—the logic, mastery, generosity, and love evidenced in every detail of life.

Have a Completely Positive Day

Ask God to walk through your day with you and help you stay completely positive. Don't say anything negative, even in jest. But go further—look for opportunities to say something positive and affirming to people who cross your path: "Good job," "Great coffee," "Nice color on you," "Such a delightful store." And say positive things to God throughout your day, too.

Learn to Walk One Step at a Time

Go on a midnight walk, and take along your flashlight. Keep the light aimed just ahead of you on the path, so that you can only see to walk a step at a time. Consider why God often gives us just enough information to allow us the next step. Instead of demanding that God answer your major dilemma—Should you move? Change jobs? Get married?—ask what your next minor step might be. Could you check the Internet for housing in other locations? Talk to a friend about another job? Discuss goals and dreams with your boyfriend or girlfriend? Trust that God will lead you, one step at a time.

Keep a God Jar

When God gives you a moment you don't want forget, jot down a note and date it: *Boss said I was irreplaceable. Wife called to say she loved me. I won the tennis match. Saw three deer on the drive home. Daughter said I was the best mom. Grandson took his first step.* Keep your notes in a jar. You can pull out your God Jar any time and thank God all over again. Remember that God is the same now as he was then.

Enjoy God the Father

List the ways a parent loves a child—protects that child from danger, sacrifices, delights in the child's little successes, teaches, guides and directs, is concerned about the child's future. Include the things parents do for their kids—such as creating a sense of fun and saying no to things that would be undesirable. Go through your list and thank God for being a parent to you and for loving you the way parents love their children.

70

Name that Tune!

The next time an old favorite comes on over the radio, stop and remember. But instead of just remembering the song, let the music bring back details of people, places, and things for which you can thank God. Are you thankful that God gave you those friends? Do you like the person you are now better than the struggling kid you were then? Can you see how God took care of you during a rough patch in your past? Name the tune, and name the blessings.

Imagine Heaven

Stare up at a cloud-filled sky and try to imagine what heaven is like. How do you picture it? Do you think people treat each other with kindness and consideration? Do they worship God continually and sincerely? Is there a spirit of peace and joy from working together?

As you go through your day, remember your picture of heaven and try to bring a little of heaven on earth by treating others the way you visualized people are treated in heaven.

72

Shower Talk with God

Take a long, hot shower and talk to God about
the joys of being alone at times, and knowing
you are never completely alone; God is there.
As the water washes and the steam rises,
meditate on the amazing grace of God's
presence that surrounds us, even when we
may think we're all alone in the shower.

Let God carry the Burden

Instead of worrying about the people you love
and picturing the worst things that could
happen to them, try handing them over to God.
Close your eyes and picture yourself picking up
your loved one as a child, then handing the heavy
load to God. Trust God and his loving care.

Create Your Own
Special Calendar

Go through your calendar or schedule and
randomly mark days with a symbol, such as "#."
Place your symbol to appear at least a couple
of times each month. Throughout the year,
whenever you come upon this symbol, pause
and remind yourself that days are numbered.
You'll never get this exact date back again.
Ask God to help you make it count.

75

change Your Outlook

If you wear glasses, use them to change your
spiritual outlook, as well as your physical vision.
Each time you put on your glasses, ask God to give
you a godly view of everything you see. Look past
grouchiness to see if someone is in pain. Get
beyond the way people dress or their physical
appearance. If you don't wear glasses, you can
change your outlook with sunglasses. And every
time you see someone else put on glasses, ask God
to help you adjust your own vision.

Drive-Thru Blessing

Appoint each routine drive as a time to bless someone through prayer. Talk to God about the person, using the acronym BLESS: B—Body (physical protection); L—Love (feel the love of God today; confident in your love or friendship); E—Emotional (for this person's feelings and well-being); S—Sight (see things through God's eyes); S—Spiritual (for spiritual needs and growth). Give drive-thru blessings to a different person each day of the week.

Take a Deep Breath and Count to Ten

At stressful moments throughout the day,
take a deep breath and hold it as long as you
can. But instead of just counting to ten,
consider all the parts of your body that keep
on working without your conscious help.
Appreciate the intricacies of your heart, the
blood system, your organs, all set by God to
automatically keep you going. Thank God for
your very life and breath—and let the air out.

Imagine the Potter

Take a lump of clay (you can use play dough)
and try to make something. As you change the
shape and mold the clay, talk to God, the Potter,
who works on you, enjoying your growth and
transformation. Can you identify areas on which
God may still be working—commitment,
integrity, discipline? What could you do to help—
Write out a schedule? Stop pilfering supplies?
Set the alarm fifteen minutes earlier?

Paper Prayer

As you read through the newspaper today, let
God touch your heart with godly compassion
for the tragedies and problems you read about.
Pray for these people whose lives will never
physically touch yours. Realize that we're all
part of the same family, God's family; and pray
for God's peace, justice, and order.

80

Back to Life's Basics

Clean out your closets, garage, or attic.
Rid yourself of stuff you don't use. Give it away,
or toss it. When you're done, celebrate with
a simple meal of crusty bread, cheese, and fruit.
Ask God to help you live an unfettered life.
And thank God for your daily bread.

81

Believe Without Seeing

List ten things you believe in without
seeing—Neptune, electricity, oxygen, wind, love,
marriage. Reaffirm to God your belief and faith
in God and the things of God. Talk to God about
all the things you believe, even though you
cannot touch or see them—love, goodness,
kindness, faithfulness, joy, peace, God.

Unselfish Joy

Thank God for the blessings God has given an acquaintance or a loved one—a good family, a job, a new home. Experience the joy of unselfishly being happy for someone else. It beats jealousy! If appropriate, and you're sincere, tell that person how happy you are for his or her blessing. And thank God for caring for someone else.

83

Catch People in an Act of God

For one whole day, go on a good-deed hunt.
Pay attention to the thoughtful and kind
things people do for each other. Whenever
possible, express your appreciation and respect.
Thank God for the everyday kindness and goodness
that go on around us, often unnoticed.

84

Holding Hands with God

Invite a neighbor in your house of worship to
hold hands. Be grateful to God that you know
someone whose hand you can hold on to. And
thank God for never letting go of *your* hand.

Give Flowers on an Ordinary Day

Buy or pick flowers for someone for no reason at all. Select a day that's not a birthday or holiday, not a day when you need to apologize. Then give your flowers to your friend. Thank God for God's grace, freely given and totally undeserved.

Create Your Own Black-out

Declare a black-out night—no TV, radio, or
CD-player. Take the phone off the hook. Enjoy
reading by candlelight or sitting and talking. In the
absence of noise and the usual distractions, let
your heart be still and commune with God,
throughout the whole evening.

87

Hide a Surprise

Surprise someone with an encouraging note
or a verse from the Bible. Hide the note in
a lunchbox, in the car, or on a desk. Then
hide another note thanking God for encouraging
you. Each time you run across the note, give
God thanks one more time.

88

Do Something You Hate

Do something you hate with someone you love.
Go to a ballgame or go shopping. Play someone
else's game—Monopoly, poker, basketball,
air hockey, or a word game. Ask God to help
you enjoy the experience and to reveal new things
that you can love about your friend.

Include Someone

Prayerfully be on the lookout for people who are subtly excluded. Draw them into your conversations. Ask for their opinions, and listen to their answers. Let them know you value what they have to contribute. Thank God that you can feel valued since you have been invited into God's presence and asked to talk whenever you want to.

Be Flexible

On a Monday morning, ask God to make you flexible. Then during the day, be in prayer and open to any change God might have in mind. Be willing to alter your routine or your plans for the day—to eat lunch with someone instead of eating alone, to visit a sick friend rather than going straight home after work, to go for a walk instead of watching TV at night. Try to stay tuned-in, moment-by-moment, for God's guidance.

Four Letters that Lead to God

Take a few minutes to be alone with God.
Organize your thoughts and conversation with
God by praying the "ACTS":

A=Adoration: Express your love for God,
                    and tell God why you do.

C=Confession: Confess, or agree
                    with God about your sins.

T=Thanksgiving: Thank God for
                    specific gifts, for people.

S=Supplication: Last, ask God for
                    specific needs and desires.

Spin 'til You're Upright

Spin in a circle five times fast; then stop. As you
recover your equilibrium, admit to God areas
where your life may be out of balance—too
much work, too little family time, poor eating
or health habits, unhealthy relationships. Talk
to God about righting yourself, making the
adjustments that will restore balance—a new
division of your free time, diet and exercise.

Spend a Day in the Back Seat

For a full day, actively put other people ahead
of yourself. Let merging drivers in. Give up
a parking spot. Go to the back of the line.
Get coffee or run errands for people who
generally do so for you. Talk to God about
your feelings as you put the needs or wishes
of others ahead of your own desires.

Rope in the Last Waking Moment

When you climb into bed and snuggle under the covers, give God your conscious thought. With the lights out, thank God for one thing that happened during the day. Imagine twirling a lariat over your pillow and roping in one situation you'll face tomorrow. Round it up, and bring it in to God. Finally, don't forget to tell God goodnight.

95

Zero In

Talk to God about your biggest vice—drinking,
gossiping, being jealous and envious, lying.
Write down why this is your major offense.
Include all the details. Place your list in a box
and wrap the box. Give your vice to God, a gift.
Store the box in your closet. Bring it out on your
birthday and talk to God about how you're doing.

Tie a String Around Your Finger

If you tend to forget about God during your busy day, you need to remind yourself to talk to God. An actual string around your finger may be too obvious, but find another reminder that works for you. When another person says hello, return the greeting, and let it remind you to greet God, to thank God for going with you wherever you go. Or, at the beginning of each break, let that be your signal to talk to God about whatever is on your mind. Find your own version of the string around the finger.

Scribe for God

Imagine what God might say to you in a letter. Then write that letter as if you were God. Express love and approval. Give directions and orders. Point out things in your life that need changing. Write down what is loveable about you—Your laugh? Your sense of humor? Your concern? Let God ask you questions. And when you're all done, address the letter to yourself, and sign it: "Love, God." The next day, answer God's letter.

Smile to a stranger

Step out of yourself and smile at strangers
throughout the day. See how many people you
can get to return your smile. Don't be upset
when you don't get a smile in return. You'll
get your smile back from God.

This Way Up

When you step into an elevator, imagine you're
placing yourself in God's palm. Ask God to lift
your spirits as you take the elevator up.
Sense God's presence. Ask God to help you
lift the spirits of one person today.

Bike It!

Take a long, leisurely bike ride. Talk to God
about the feeling of freedom. Rejoice in
the freedom you have to ride wherever you please,
to enjoy flowers and countryside. If you know
you need to get yourself in better shape, now's
the time to work out the details before God.
Commit yourself to a plan of regular exercise
and diet; and ask God to help you do it!

Dance With God

When nobody's around to make fun, put on
your favorite dancing music—loud. Dance
until you feel your inhibitions fall away.
Close your eyes and let your soul and body praise
God for the life you've been given. Imagine
God watching or joining you. Dance for joy!

About the Author

Dandi Daley Mackall is the author of over 200 children's books and 27 books for adults, including *God Made Me* (in its tenth printing) and *Kids Say the Greatest Things About God*. Her books have sold more than one million copies. She writes from rural Ohio, where she lives with her husband, her three children, two horses, a dog, and a cat.